The Mindset for Living in a World with Artificial Intelligence

Warren Brown

Published by Warren Brown, 2023.

THE MINDSET FOR LIVING IN A WORLD WITH ARTIFICIAL INTELLIGENCE

First edition. April 23, 2023.

Copyright © 2023 Warren Brown.

ISBN: 979-8223048046

Written by Warren Brown.

Also by Warren Brown

Prolific Writing for Everyone
On Writing Magic
The Writer's Creativity Cave
The Writer's Oasis
Castle of Ideas and Inspiration for Writers
Chasm of Creativity and Inspiration For Writers
Island of Creativity and Inspiration for Writers

Standalone
Supernova: A Collection of Science Fiction Short Stories
Instant Poetry App
The Power of the Storyteller- A Collection of Short Stories
Vintage Tales: Eurasian Short Stories
Impostor Assassin
Camelot Crypto 1- Crypto Genesis
Camelot Crypto 2- Crypto Odyssey
Camelot Crypto 3- Crypto Symbiosis
Camelot Crypto: Three Short Crypto-currency Stories
Three Christmas Coins: A Poem
The Christmas Dimension
Happy New Year
Festive Delights

Coulrophobia: Empire of the Clown King
Creative Vibes
Rewrite Your Story To Become The Hero
Pandemic Blasters
New Year Odyssey
Pandemic Blasters Omnibus
Travel Man
Monkey in Mind
Masquerade
The Marauders and Mavericks
Mystic Inspiration Prompts for Writers
Cafe of Creativity and Inspiration For Writers
Quick Guide to Increasing Sales for Your Magnetic E-Book
The Global Citizen: A Step-by-Step Guide to Living, Working, and
Thriving Anywhere in the World
The Mindset for Living in a World with Artificial Intelligence

Watch for more at https://warren4.wixsite.com/warren.

Table of Contents

The Mindset for Living in a World with Artificial Intelligence

Effective A.I. Evolution

By

Warren Brown

**GOLDCOPY INDEPENDENT PUBLISHING
LONDON. UNITED KINGDOM. 2023**

Title: The Mindset for Living in a World with Artificial Intelligence
Subtitle: Effective A.I. Evolution
Author: Warren Brown
Copyright @Warren Brown. London. United Kingdom. 2023
Cover: Created in Canva by Warren Brown, with AI generated art.
Date: 23 April 2023

Introduction

"How to develop the Ideal Mindset for 21st Century Living". The book focusses on a number of issues, starting from, your present state of mind, the ideal state of mind for this day and age, how we view work, how we view life, how we view love, how we view death now. We are presented with the ideal state of mind of how we as humans need to view life, work, love, death in the 21st century. Suggested steps are, meditation techniques, plans of action about how every man, woman and child today, can change their old mindsets and evolve to living with new mindsets in the 21st century, where science, technology and industries are advancing with the assistance of AI technology. This book concludes with key points that need to be kept in mind for the future and how every individual can improve themselves in the future, with the cooperation of AI technology, while evolving as more caring, loving, understanding, charitable and tolerant human beings.

The 21st century has brought unprecedented changes and advancements in science, technology, and industry. With the help of AI technology, we have made remarkable progress in fields such as medicine, communication, and transportation. However, with these advancements comes the need for us as individuals to evolve and adapt our mindsets to keep up with the ever-changing world around us. The purpose of this book is to provide you with the tools and knowledge needed to develop the ideal mindset for 21st century living. We will explore topics such as understanding your current state of mind, the ideal state of mind for this day and age, redefining work, embracing life, reimagining love, and understanding death. We will also discuss the role of AI technology in our mindset evolution, the impact of technology on our mindset, and the importance of mindfulness, emotional intelligence, and self-care. By the end of this book, you will have a clear understanding of how to change your old mindset and evolve into a more caring, loving, understanding, charitable, and tolerant human being. You will have the tools and knowledge needed to develop a growth mindset for lifelong learning, achieve your goals, and build a more compassionate and tolerant society.

In the fast-paced world of the 21st century, it is more important than ever to develop an ideal mindset. The way we think about life, work, love, and death has a significant impact on our overall well-being and success. With the constant advancements in science, technology, and AI, it is essential to adapt and evolve our mindsets to keep up with the times.

Mindset Evolution is a comprehensive guide to developing the ideal mindset for 21st century living. In this book, you will learn about the current state of your mindset and the changes needed to thrive in this new era. You will discover the ideal mindset for success in the modern world, with a focus on redefining work, embracing life, reimagining love, and understanding death.

The book also covers the science of mindset, the impact of technology on our thinking, and the importance of mindfulness, meditation, and emotional intelligence in developing the ideal mindset. You will find practical techniques for developing resilience, self-care, and a growth mindset, as well as a plan of action for developing the ideal mindset.

Finally, the book explores the impact of AI on mindset evolution and how we can evolve as more caring, loving, understanding, charitable, and tolerant human beings. By the end of this book, you will have the tools to change your old mindset and develop a new one that will help you thrive in the 21st century.

Chapter 1: Your Present State of Mind: Understanding Your Mindset

Your mindset is the collection of beliefs, attitudes, and assumptions that shape the way you perceive the world around you. It influences your thoughts, emotions, and behaviours, and plays a significant role in determining your level of success and happiness in life. Understanding your current mindset is the first step in developing the ideal mindset for the 21st century.

Types of Mindsets

There are two main types of mindsets: fixed and growth. A fixed mindset is a belief that your qualities and abilities are set in stone and cannot be changed. People with a fixed mindset tend to avoid challenges, give up easily, and view effort as a sign of weakness. They also tend to compare themselves to others and feel threatened by the success of others.

On the other hand, a growth mindset is a belief that your qualities and abilities can be developed through dedication and hard work. People with a growth mindset embrace challenges, persist in the face of obstacles, and see effort as a path to mastery. They also celebrate the success of others and see it as an opportunity to learn.

Limiting Beliefs

Limiting beliefs are deeply held beliefs about ourselves and the world that hold us back from reaching our full potential. These beliefs are often formed in childhood and can be reinforced by negative experiences or self-talk. Some common limiting beliefs include "I'm not smart enough," "I don't deserve success," and "I'll never be able to change."

Limiting beliefs can be identified by paying attention to your self-talk and the stories you tell yourself about your abilities and potential. By becoming aware of your limiting beliefs, you can challenge them and replace them with more empowering beliefs that support your growth and success.

Changing Your Mindset

Changing your mindset requires a conscious effort to challenge your existing beliefs and replace them with more empowering ones. This involves developing self-awareness, setting goals, and taking action towards those goals.

Self-awareness is the foundation of mindset change. It involves becoming aware of your thoughts, emotions, and behaviors and understanding how they are influenced by your beliefs and assumptions. Self-awareness can be developed through mindfulness practices, such as meditation or journaling.

Setting goals is also essential in changing your mindset. Goals provide direction and purpose and help you focus your efforts on what is important. They also help you measure progress and celebrate your successes. When setting goals, it's important to make them specific, measurable, achievable, relevant, and time-bound (SMART).

Taking action towards your goals is the final step in changing your mindset. This involves stepping outside of your comfort zone, taking risks, and persisting in the face of obstacles. It also involves seeking feedback and learning from your mistakes.

Conclusion

Understanding your current mindset is the first step in developing the ideal mindset for the 21st century. By identifying your limiting beliefs and replacing them with more empowering ones, you can cultivate a growth mindset that supports your personal and professional growth. Developing self-awareness, setting goals, and taking action towards those goals are key steps in changing your mindset and achieving success in all areas of your life.

Chapter 2: The Ideal State of Mind for the 21st Century

The 21st century is a time of rapid change and unprecedented challenges. To navigate this complex and ever-evolving world, we need an ideal state of mind that allows us to thrive both personally and professionally. In this chapter, we will explore the characteristics of the ideal state of mind for the 21st century.

1. Growth Mindset: The ideal state of mind is one that is growth-oriented, where we see challenges as opportunities for learning and development. A growth mindset is characterized by a willingness to embrace new ideas and experiences, a desire to learn from failure, and a belief in our own ability to improve and grow.

2. Adaptability: The ideal state of mind is one that is adaptable, where we are able to adjust to changing circumstances and embrace new opportunities. In a world where technology and social norms are constantly evolving, adaptability is crucial for success.

3. Resilience: The ideal state of mind is one that is resilient, where we are able to bounce back from setbacks and persevere in the face of adversity. Resilience allows us to maintain our focus and motivation even when things get tough.

4. Emotional Intelligence: The ideal state of mind is one that is

emotionally intelligent, where we are able to understand and manage our own emotions and empathize with others. Emotional intelligence is critical for building strong relationships and navigating complex social situations.

5. Mindfulness: The ideal state of mind is one that is mindful, where we are fully present and engaged in the present moment. Mindfulness allows us to reduce stress, increase focus, and cultivate a sense of calm and clarity.

6. Creativity: The ideal state of mind is one that is creative, where we are able to generate new ideas and solutions to complex problems. Creativity allows us to think outside the box and approach challenges with a fresh perspective.

7. Purpose: The ideal state of mind is one that is driven by purpose, where we have a clear sense of our values and goals. Purpose gives us direction and meaning, and allows us to stay motivated and focused on what truly matters.

Conclusion

By cultivating these characteristics in our own minds, we can develop the ideal state of mind for the 21st century. With this ideal mindset, we are better equipped to navigate the challenges of the modern world and create a meaningful and fulfilling life.

Chapter 3: Redefining Work: How to View Your Career in the Modern Age

The nature of work has changed significantly in recent years, and traditional notions of a stable, linear career path have become increasingly outdated. In the 21st century, work is no longer just a means of earning a living but also a source of personal fulfilment and meaning. In this chapter, we will explore how to view your career in the modern age and the steps you can take to succeed in today's ever-evolving job market.

1. Embrace the Gig Economy: The gig economy has emerged as a popular alternative to traditional employment, with more and more people opting for freelance or contract work. This allows individuals to have greater flexibility in their work arrangements and pursue multiple career paths simultaneously. Embracing the gig economy can be a viable option for those looking to create their own career paths and take control of their professional lives.

2. Continuously Learn and Upskill: The rapid pace of technological advancement means that skills can quickly become obsolete. To stay relevant in the job market, it is crucial to continuously learn and upskill. This can involve taking courses, attending workshops, or pursuing additional certifications. By staying up-to-date with the latest industry trends, you can position yourself as a valuable asset to any

organization.

3. Focus on Transferable Skills: While technical skills are important, many employers now prioritize transferable skills such as communication, problem-solving, and teamwork. These skills can be applied across various industries and are highly sought after in today's job market. Focusing on developing these skills can enhance your employability and make you more adaptable to changing career demands.

4. Pursue Your Passion: With the rise of remote work and flexible schedules, more and more people are turning their passions into viable careers. By pursuing work that aligns with your interests and values, you can find greater fulfilment and purpose in your professional life. This can involve starting your own business, freelancing, or pursuing a non-traditional career path.

5. Adopt an Entrepreneurial Mindset: The traditional notion of a career for life no longer applies in the 21st century. Adopting an entrepreneurial mindset can help you navigate the uncertainty of the job market and create your own career opportunities. This involves being proactive, taking calculated risks, and constantly seeking out new opportunities for growth and development.

In conclusion, the modern age presents a wealth of opportunities for those willing to adapt to the changing nature of work. By embracing the gig economy, continuously learning and upskilling, focusing on transferable skills, pursuing your passions, and adopting an entrepreneurial mindset, you can redefine your career and achieve success in the 21st century job market.

Chapter 4: Embracing Life: Developing a Positive and Growth-Oriented Mindset

Life is full of challenges, but it is also full of opportunities. The way we approach life has a significant impact on our well-being and happiness. A positive and growth-oriented mindset can help us embrace life and all it has to offer.

In this chapter, we will explore how to develop a positive and growth-oriented mindset. We will discuss the benefits of adopting this mindset and how it can help us overcome obstacles and achieve our goals. We will also examine the importance of cultivating gratitude and practicing mindfulness in our daily lives.

Developing a positive mindset involves shifting our focus from negative to positive thoughts. Instead of dwelling on problems, we can focus on finding solutions. By developing a growth-oriented mindset, we can view challenges as opportunities for learning and personal growth. We can develop resilience and the ability to bounce back from setbacks.

Cultivating gratitude is another essential aspect of developing a positive mindset. By focusing on what we have rather than what we lack, we can increase our sense of well-being and satisfaction. Practicing mindfulness can also help us stay present in the moment and appreciate the beauty of life.

In addition to these practices, it is essential to take care of our physical and emotional well-being. Eating a healthy diet, getting regular exercise, and getting enough sleep can all contribute to a positive mindset. Engaging in activities that bring us joy and fulfilment can also increase our sense of happiness and well-being.

In conclusion, developing a positive and growth-oriented mindset is essential for embracing life and all it has to offer. By shifting our focus to positive thoughts, cultivating gratitude, and practicing mindfulness, we can develop resilience and the ability to overcome challenges. Taking care of our physical and emotional well-being is also critical for maintaining a positive mindset. With these practices, we can embrace life with open arms and achieve our goals.

Chapter 5: Reimagining Love: Building Healthy and Meaningful Relationships

Love is an essential part of the human experience, and building healthy and meaningful relationships is crucial for our well-being. However, traditional ideas of love and relationships have been challenged in recent years, with new models of love emerging that prioritize mutual respect, communication, and personal growth.

In this chapter, we will explore some of these new models and discuss how we can reimagine love to build healthier and more meaningful relationships. We will discuss the importance of self-love and how it impacts our ability to love others. We will also delve into the concept of "conscious relationships," which emphasize personal growth, open communication, and mutual respect.

One key aspect of building healthy relationships is communication. It is essential to learn how to communicate effectively with your partner, friends, and family. This involves active listening, expressing your thoughts and feelings clearly, and being open to feedback. It is also important to set boundaries and respect the boundaries of others.

Another aspect of building healthy relationships is personal growth. It is essential to recognize that we are constantly evolving and changing, and our relationships must adapt and grow with us. This means being willing to challenge our own beliefs and assumptions, being open to new experiences, and supporting our partner's growth and development.

We will also discuss the importance of forgiveness and letting go of past hurts in building healthy relationships. Holding onto resentment and anger can poison a relationship, so it is essential to learn how to forgive and move forward.

Finally, we will explore the concept of "radical acceptance," which involves accepting our partners for who they are, flaws and all. This means recognizing that no one is perfect, and focusing on the positive aspects of our partner rather than dwelling on their shortcomings.

In conclusion, building healthy and meaningful relationships requires a shift in mindset towards mutual respect, communication, and personal growth. By reimagining love and adopting new models of relationships, we can cultivate deeper connections with our partners and experience greater happiness and fulfilment in our lives.

Chapter 6: Understanding Death: Coping with Loss and Embracing Change

Death is an inevitable part of life, yet many of us struggle to cope with it. Whether it is the loss of a loved one or the realization of our own mortality, death can evoke a range of emotions from fear and sadness to anger and confusion. However, by understanding death and learning to embrace it, we can develop a deeper appreciation for life and the time we have.

In this chapter, we will explore the different aspects of death and how to cope with loss. We will discuss the various stages of grief and the importance of allowing yourself to feel and express your emotions. We will also examine the role of acceptance and how it can help you move forward in life.

Moreover, we will discuss the concept of death positivity, which involves embracing death as a natural and inevitable part of life. By changing our perspective on death, we can learn to celebrate life and appreciate the time we have with loved ones.

Finally, we will also discuss the impact of death on our sense of purpose and the importance of finding meaning in life. By embracing change and finding a sense of purpose, we can turn the experience of loss into an opportunity for growth and personal transformation.

In conclusion, by understanding death and learning to cope with loss, we can develop a more positive and growth-oriented mindset. By embracing change and finding meaning in life, we can turn the experience of loss into an opportunity for personal growth and transformation.

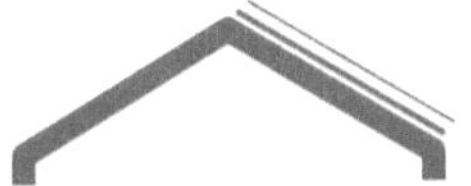

Chapter 7: The Ideal State of Mind: A Holistic View

The ideal state of mind is one that encompasses a holistic view of life. It is a state of mind that integrates various aspects of your being, including your physical, emotional, mental, and spiritual selves. A holistic approach to mindset development emphasizes the importance of balance and harmony in all areas of your life.

To achieve an ideal state of mind, it is essential to cultivate a sense of self-awareness and mindfulness. This means being present and fully engaged in the moment, without judgment or distraction. It also means being aware of your thoughts, emotions, and physical sensations and how they impact your overall well-being.

A holistic view of mindset development also includes the importance of self-care. This means taking care of your physical, emotional, and mental health through activities such as exercise, healthy eating, and stress management. It also means taking time for yourself to engage in activities that bring you joy and fulfilment.

In addition to self-care, a holistic view of mindset development includes the importance of social connection and community. This means building and maintaining healthy relationships with friends, family, and your broader community. It also means giving back and contributing to the well-being of others.

Finally, a holistic view of mindset development includes the importance of a sense of purpose and meaning in life. This means identifying and pursuing your passions, values, and goals. It also means aligning your actions with your values and contributing to something greater than yourself.

In summary, the ideal state of mind is a holistic one that encompasses self-awareness, mindfulness, self-care, social connection, and purpose. By cultivating these aspects of your being, you can achieve a sense of balance and harmony that leads to greater well-being and fulfilment in life.

Chapter 8: The Power of Positive Thinking: The Science of Mindset

The power of positive thinking has been a popular concept for decades, but it is much more than just a self-help idea. There is scientific evidence that supports the idea that positive thinking can have a significant impact on your life and well-being. In this chapter, we will explore the science behind positive thinking and how it can benefit your mindset and overall health.

Positive thinking is the practice of focusing on the good in your life and expecting positive outcomes. This mindset can lead to increased feelings of happiness, satisfaction, and overall well-being. Studies have shown that people with a positive outlook on life have lower levels of stress and are less likely to experience depression and anxiety.

Positive thinking can also have physical health benefits. Studies have shown that a positive mindset can lead to a stronger immune system, lower blood pressure, and reduced risk of chronic diseases such as cardiovascular disease.

The science behind positive thinking is based on the idea of neuroplasticity, which is the brain's ability to change and adapt. When you consistently focus on positive thoughts and emotions, you are rewiring your brain to make positive connections and associations. Over time, this can lead to a more positive outlook on life and a more optimistic mindset.

It is important to note that positive thinking does not mean ignoring negative emotions or experiences. It is about acknowledging them and choosing to focus on the positive aspects of your life. This can involve practices such as gratitude journaling, positive affirmations, and surrounding yourself with positive people and environments.

In summary, the power of positive thinking is supported by scientific evidence and can have a significant impact on your mindset and overall health. By focusing on the good in your life and cultivating a positive mindset, you can experience increased happiness, reduced stress, and improved physical health.

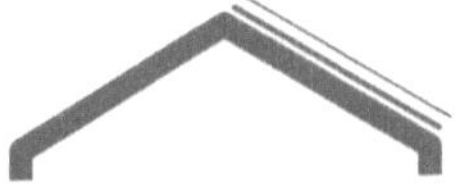

Chapter 9: The Impact of Technology on Our Mindset

Technology has been rapidly advancing in the 21st century and has had a significant impact on our lives, including our mindset. While technology has brought many benefits, such as increased connectivity and access to information, it has also led to certain challenges that can affect our mindset.

One of the major impacts of technology on our mindset is the constant need for instant gratification. With the availability of instant messaging, social media, and on-demand entertainment, we have become accustomed to immediate responses and results. This can lead to impatience, frustration, and a lack of perseverance when faced with challenges that require time and effort to overcome.

Another impact of technology is the potential for addiction. Many people have become reliant on technology, whether it is through social media, gaming, or other digital platforms, leading to a loss of control over their use of technology. This can lead to a lack of focus, decreased productivity, and even mental health issues.

Furthermore, technology can also affect our ability to communicate and connect with others. With the prevalence of social media and online communication, we may become less adept at face-to-face communication, empathy, and understanding. This can lead to feelings of isolation, disconnection, and a lack of social support.

However, technology can also have positive effects on our mindset. For example, digital tools such as meditation and mindfulness apps can help us manage stress, cultivate positive emotions, and increase our resilience. Additionally, technology can enable us to connect with others across geographic and cultural boundaries, increasing our awareness and empathy towards others.

To develop an ideal mindset in the age of technology, it is important to use technology mindfully and intentionally. This means being aware of how we use technology and the impact it has on our mindset, and making conscious choices to use technology in ways that promote growth, learning, and connection. We should also make an effort to balance our use of technology with other activities, such as face-to-face communication, physical exercise, and spending time in nature.

Overall, technology has the power to shape our mindset in both positive and negative ways. By being aware of its impact and using it intentionally, we can develop a mindset that is adaptable, resilient, and focused on growth and connection.

Chapter 10: Mindfulness and Meditation: Techniques for Developing the Ideal Mindset

Mindfulness and meditation are powerful tools for developing the ideal mindset. They help you become more aware of your thoughts and emotions, and allow you to observe them without judgment. This can lead to greater self-awareness and self-regulation, and can improve your ability to focus, reduce stress, and enhance well-being.

Mindfulness is the practice of being present in the moment, fully engaged in what you are doing without distraction. It involves paying attention to your thoughts, feelings, and physical sensations in a non-judgmental way. Meditation is a related practice that involves focusing your attention on a specific object or activity, such as your breath or a sound.

There are many different techniques and approaches to mindfulness and meditation, and it is important to find the ones that work best for you. Some common techniques include:

1. Mindful breathing: This involves focusing on your breath, noticing the sensation of air moving in and out of your body. When your mind wanders, gently bring it back to your breath.

2. Body scan: This involves slowly and mindfully scanning your body from head to toe, noticing any sensations or feelings.

3. Loving-kindness meditation: This involves cultivating feelings of compassion and kindness towards yourself and others, using phrases such as "may I be happy" or "may you be healthy."
4. Walking meditation: This involves walking mindfully, paying attention to the sensation of your feet on the ground and the movement of your body.
5. Mindful eating: This involves eating mindfully, paying attention to the taste, texture, and sensation of food, and noticing any thoughts or feelings that arise.

Research has shown that regular mindfulness and meditation practice can have a range of benefits for mental and physical health, including reducing anxiety and depression, improving sleep quality, and enhancing overall well-being.

Incorporating mindfulness and meditation into your daily routine can be a powerful way to cultivate the ideal mindset. Even just a few minutes a day can make a significant difference in your ability to manage stress, stay focused, and approach life with greater clarity and purpose.

Chapter 11: The Role of Emotional Intelligence in Developing the Ideal Mindset

Emotional intelligence (EI) is the ability to recognize and manage your own emotions, as well as those of others. Developing emotional intelligence is essential in cultivating the ideal mindset as it helps you understand and regulate your thoughts, behaviours, and actions. In this chapter, we will explore the role of emotional intelligence in developing the ideal mindset and how it can be applied in various aspects of life.

Emotional intelligence comprises four main components:

1. Self-awareness: The ability to recognize your own emotions and their impact on your thoughts and behaviors.
2. Self-regulation: The ability to control impulsive behaviors and reactions and manage your emotions effectively.
3. Social awareness: The ability to empathize with others and recognize their emotions accurately.
4. Relationship management: The ability to build and maintain healthy relationships with others.

To develop emotional intelligence, it is essential to start with self-awareness. By becoming aware of your own emotions and reactions, you can start to understand the patterns that govern your behaviour. This awareness helps you manage your emotions and regulate your responses in stressful or challenging situations.

Self-regulation is the next step in developing emotional intelligence. By managing your emotions effectively, you can avoid impulsive behaviours and maintain a level-headed approach to problem-solving. This can be especially helpful in situations where a quick, emotional response can lead to negative outcomes.

Social awareness and relationship management are the final components of emotional intelligence. Social awareness involves recognizing and understanding the emotions of others. By doing so, you can develop empathy and build stronger relationships with those around you. Relationship management involves using your emotional intelligence to build and maintain healthy relationships with others. This includes effective communication, conflict resolution, and teamwork.

Overall, emotional intelligence plays a crucial role in developing the ideal mindset. By cultivating emotional intelligence, you can develop a greater sense of self-awareness, self-regulation, social awareness, and relationship management. This, in turn, can lead to a more positive and growth-oriented mindset that is essential in the 21st century.

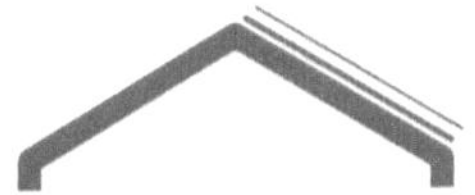

Chapter 12: Cultivating Resilience: Overcoming Adversity and Building Mental Toughness

In life, we all face challenges and setbacks, which can be emotionally and mentally draining. Resilience is the ability to adapt and bounce back from these difficulties, and it is an essential trait for developing the ideal mindset. Cultivating resilience can help you overcome adversity, build mental toughness, and maintain a positive outlook on life.

There are several ways to cultivate resilience. One is to reframe negative situations and look for the positives. This means focusing on what you can learn and how you can grow from a difficult experience rather than dwelling on the negative aspects. It can also help to seek support from friends, family, or a therapist to process your emotions and gain perspective.

Another way to build resilience is to develop a growth mindset, as we discussed earlier. This involves seeing challenges as opportunities for growth rather than as insurmountable obstacles. By embracing a growth mindset, you can view setbacks as learning experiences and use them to become stronger and more resilient.

Practicing self-care is also crucial for cultivating resilience. Taking care of your physical, emotional, and mental well-being can help you stay grounded and maintain your inner strength. This can include getting enough sleep, eating well, exercising regularly, and engaging in activities that bring you joy and relaxation.

Finally, it's important to remember that resilience is not something you develop overnight. It takes time, effort, and practice. By embracing a growth mindset, seeking support, practicing self-care, and reframing negative situations, you can cultivate resilience and build mental toughness, which will serve you well in all areas of life.

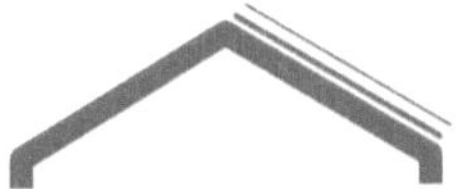

Chapter 13: The Importance of Self-Care in Developing the Ideal Mindset

In today's fast-paced and busy world, it is easy to neglect our own well-being. However, taking care of ourselves is essential for developing the ideal mindset. Self-care is the practice of prioritizing our physical, emotional, and mental health needs.

In this chapter, we will explore the importance of self-care in developing the ideal mindset. We will discuss the different areas of self-care, including physical, emotional, and mental self-care. We will also explore the benefits of self-care and how it can help us become more productive, focused, and resilient.

Physical self-care includes activities such as getting enough sleep, eating a healthy diet, and engaging in regular exercise. When we take care of our physical needs, we have more energy and are better able to cope with stress.

Emotional self-care involves activities such as spending time with loved ones, engaging in hobbies, and practicing self-compassion. When we take care of our emotional needs, we are better able to regulate our emotions and maintain positive relationships.

Mental self-care includes activities such as practicing mindfulness, journaling, and seeking professional help when needed. When we take care of our mental health, we are better able to handle stress and maintain a positive outlook.

Self-care is not selfish; it is an essential aspect of developing the ideal mindset. By prioritizing our own well-being, we are better able to serve others and achieve our goals. Taking care of ourselves allows us to be more present, focused, and productive in all aspects of our lives.

In summary, self-care is crucial for developing the ideal mindset. It includes physical, emotional, and mental self-care and is essential for maintaining our well-being. By prioritizing self-care, we can become more resilient, focused, and productive in all areas of our lives.

Chapter 14: A Plan of Action: Steps for Developing the Ideal Mindset

Developing the ideal mindset is not an overnight process, but rather a journey that requires consistent effort and commitment. In this chapter, we will discuss some practical steps that you can take to develop the ideal mindset for success and well-being.

Step 1: Self-awareness The first step towards developing the ideal mindset is to become self-aware. This involves understanding your current mindset, identifying your strengths and weaknesses, and recognizing the areas that require improvement. Self-awareness allows you to take control of your thoughts and emotions, enabling you to develop a more positive and growth-oriented mindset.

Step 2: Mindset Shift Once you have identified your current mindset, the next step is to shift your mindset. This involves challenging your limiting beliefs and replacing them with positive and empowering beliefs. You can do this by reframing your thoughts, focusing on your strengths, and practicing gratitude. A growth mindset that focuses on learning and improvement is essential for developing the ideal mindset.

Step 3: Emotional Regulation Emotional regulation is the ability to manage your emotions effectively. This involves developing skills such as mindfulness, deep breathing, and visualization. These techniques can help you to control your emotions and respond to stressful situations in a positive and productive manner.

Step 4: Positive Self-Talk Positive self-talk involves replacing negative self-talk with positive and empowering statements. This can help you to build self-confidence, increase your motivation, and develop a more positive outlook on life. Practice positive self-talk by affirming yourself with positive statements and avoiding self-criticism.

Step 5: Personal Development Personal development is an ongoing process of self-improvement. This involves setting goals, developing skills, and acquiring knowledge that can help you to achieve your full potential. Focus on developing skills that align with your values and goals, and seek out opportunities for learning and growth.

Step 6: Self-care is essential for developing the ideal mindset. This involves taking care of your physical, mental, and emotional health. Practice self-care by getting enough sleep, eating a healthy diet, exercising regularly, and engaging in activities that bring you joy and relaxation.

In conclusion, developing the ideal mindset requires consistent effort and commitment. By practicing self-awareness, shifting your mindset, regulating your emotions, engaging in positive self-talk, focusing on personal development, and practicing self-care, you can develop a mindset that is aligned with your values and goals, and that promotes well-being and success.

Chapter 15: The Impact of AI on Mindset Evolution

Artificial Intelligence (AI) is rapidly transforming various aspects of our lives, including how we work, communicate, and even think. As AI technology advances, it is crucial to understand its impact on our mindset and how we can adapt to this new reality. In this chapter, we will discuss the ways in which AI is influencing our mindset evolution.

One significant way that AI is affecting our mindset is by changing the way we perceive intelligence. Traditionally, intelligence has been associated with logical reasoning and problem-solving skills, which are often attributed to human beings. However, with the advent of AI, machines are increasingly demonstrating these skills, challenging our traditional understanding of intelligence. As a result, our mindset is evolving to incorporate the idea that intelligence can exist beyond human capabilities.

AI is also influencing our mindset in terms of how we approach decision-making. With the ability to process vast amounts of data quickly and efficiently, AI is becoming a valuable tool for decision-making in various industries, including finance, healthcare, and manufacturing. As a result, our mindset is shifting to incorporate the idea that data-driven decision-making is more effective than relying solely on human intuition.

Another way in which AI is impacting our mindset is by changing the way we work. With the automation of certain tasks, many jobs are becoming obsolete, leading to concerns about job security and the future of work. This is causing a shift in mindset towards embracing lifelong learning and acquiring new skills to remain relevant in the workforce.

Moreover, the use of AI is also affecting our mindset when it comes to privacy and security. As AI algorithms become more advanced, they can collect and analyse vast amounts of data from individuals, raising concerns about privacy and potential misuse of personal information. This is leading to a mindset shift towards prioritizing data protection and privacy.

In addition to these specific impacts, the increased use of AI is also contributing to a broader mindset shift towards innovation and progress. As more industries adopt AI technology, there is a growing sense that we are on the brink of a new era of unprecedented innovation and progress. This mindset is fuelling investment and research in AI technology, with the potential for significant advancements in fields such as healthcare, transportation, and energy.

However, as with any technological advancement, there are also concerns about the potential negative consequences of AI. These include the potential for job displacement, biases in AI algorithms, and the possibility of AI replacing human decision-making altogether. To ensure that AI has a positive impact on our mindset evolution, it is essential to address these concerns and develop responsible and ethical AI practices.

In conclusion, the impact of AI on our mindset evolution is significant and far-reaching. As AI technology continues to advance, it is crucial to be aware of how it is changing the way we perceive intelligence, approach decision-making, work, and value privacy and security. By embracing a growth mindset and adopting responsible and ethical AI practices, we can ensure that AI has a positive impact on our mindset evolution and contributes to a better future for all.

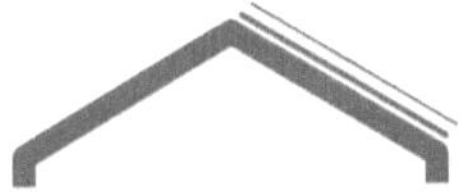

Chapter 16: Evolving as Caring and Loving Human Beings: The Future of Mindset Development

As we continue to evolve in the 21st century, it is becoming increasingly important to develop a mindset that emphasizes caring and love towards ourselves and others. This mindset is essential for building a more compassionate and tolerant society. In this chapter, we will explore the steps and plans for developing this mindset.

Step 1: Self-Reflection

The first step in developing a caring and loving mindset is self-reflection. It is important to understand our own values, beliefs, and attitudes towards ourselves and others. We can do this by asking ourselves questions such as:

- How do I treat myself when I make a mistake?
- How do I treat others when they make a mistake?
- How do I handle conflicts with others?
- How do I show empathy towards others?
- How do I show gratitude towards others?

By answering these questions honestly, we can identify areas where we need to improve our mindset and behaviour.

Step 2: Practicing Self-Compassion

Developing a caring and loving mindset starts with treating ourselves with kindness and compassion. This means acknowledging our mistakes and shortcomings without judgment or self-criticism. We can practice self-compassion by:

- Treating ourselves with the same kindness and understanding that we would offer to a good friend who is going through a difficult time.
- Recognizing that we are not alone in our struggles and that they are a natural part of the human experience.
- Practicing mindfulness to stay present and non-judgmental towards our thoughts and feelings.

Step 3: Practicing Empathy

Empathy is the ability to understand and share the feelings of others. It is a critical component of developing a caring and loving mindset. We can practice empathy by:

- Listening actively to others and seeking to understand their perspective without judgment.
- Putting ourselves in their shoes and imagining how they might be feeling.
- Expressing compassion and kindness towards others, especially when they are going through a difficult time.

Step 4: Practicing Gratitude

Gratitude is the practice of acknowledging and appreciating the good things in our lives. It is an essential component of a caring and loving mindset. We can practice gratitude by:

- Taking time each day to reflect on the good things in our lives and express gratitude for them.
- Showing appreciation towards others for their kindness and support.
- Focusing on the positive aspects of our lives, even in difficult

times.

Step 5: Building Meaningful Relationships
Developing a caring and loving mindset also involves building meaningful relationships with others. This means investing time and energy into our relationships and treating others with kindness and respect. We can build meaningful relationships by:

- Being present and attentive when we are with others.
- Showing interest in their lives and experiences.
- Offering our support and help when needed.
- Expressing our love and appreciation towards them regularly.

Step 6: Contributing to Society
Finally, developing a caring and loving mindset involves contributing to society in meaningful ways. This means using our talents and resources to make a positive impact on the world around us. We can contribute to society by:

- Volunteering our time and resources to help those in need.
- Supporting causes that are important to us.
- Being kind and compassionate towards others, even in small ways.
- Being a positive influence in our communities and workplaces.

Conclusion
Developing a caring and loving mindset is essential for building a more compassionate and tolerant society. By following these steps and plans, we can cultivate a mindset that emphasizes self-compassion, empathy, gratitude, meaningful relationships, and contribution to society. It is an ongoing process, but the benefits are immeasurable.

Chapter 17: Key Points for the Future: A Summary of Mindset Evolution

Throughout this book, we have explored various aspects of mindset development and evolution. From understanding the importance of self-awareness and emotional intelligence to the impact of technology and AI, we have covered a wide range of topics.

Here are some key points to keep in mind for the future of mindset evolution:

1. Mindset is not fixed and can be developed and changed over time.
2. A growth mindset is essential for personal and professional success, and it can be cultivated through self-awareness, positive thinking, and resilience.
3. Emotional intelligence plays a crucial role in developing a positive and growth-oriented mindset. It involves being aware of and managing your emotions and understanding the emotions of others.
4. Technology and AI have the potential to impact our mindset and the way we approach work and life. It is essential to stay informed about these changes and adapt accordingly.
5. Mindfulness and meditation can be powerful tools for developing the ideal mindset. These practices can help you manage stress, improve focus and concentration, and increase self-awareness.

6. Self-care is crucial for developing and maintaining a healthy mindset. It involves taking care of your physical, emotional, and mental well-being.
7. Developing a caring and loving mindset is crucial for building a more compassionate and tolerant society. This involves treating others with kindness and empathy and promoting inclusivity and diversity.
8. In the future, it is essential to continue learning and growing, as the world is constantly changing, and our mindset needs to evolve with it.

In conclusion, mindset evolution is an ongoing process that requires self-awareness, resilience, and a growth-oriented attitude. By cultivating a positive and growth-oriented mindset, we can achieve personal and professional success and contribute to building a better world.

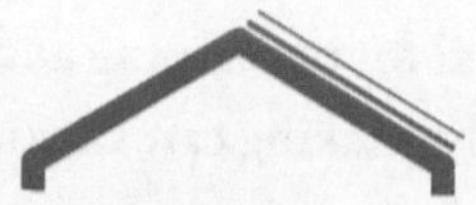

Chapter 18: Developing a Growth Mindset for Lifelong Learning- a practical step-by-step Guide

A growth mindset is a powerful tool for lifelong learning. It enables you to embrace challenges, persist in the face of obstacles, and continuously learn and grow. In this chapter, we will provide you with a step-by-step guide to developing a growth mindset for lifelong learning.

Step 1: Recognize the difference between a fixed mindset and a growth mindset The first step to developing a growth mindset is to understand the difference between a fixed mindset and a growth mindset. A fixed mindset assumes that your abilities and intelligence are fixed traits that cannot be changed. In contrast, a growth mindset assumes that your abilities and intelligence can be developed through effort, learning, and perseverance.

Step 2: Cultivate a love of learning to develop a growth mindset, you must cultivate a love of learning. Embrace new challenges, seek out new experiences, and be open to new ideas. Embrace your mistakes and failures as opportunities for growth and learning.

Step 3: Embrace challenges Challenge yourself to try new things, take risks, and step outside of your comfort zone. Recognize that challenges are opportunities to learn and grow.

Step 4: Persist in the face of obstacles When faced with obstacles, persist and persevere. Recognize that setbacks and failures are part of the learning process and that they can provide valuable feedback for improvement.

Step 5: View criticism as feedback View criticism as feedback rather than personal attacks. Embrace constructive criticism as an opportunity to learn and grow.

Step 6: Surround yourself with positive influences Surround yourself with people who support and encourage your growth. Seek out mentors, coaches, and peers who share your love of learning and growth mindset.

Step 7: Continuously learn and adapt Finally, commit to continuously learning and adapting. Develop a habit of seeking out new information, skills, and experiences. Embrace change and be open to new opportunities for growth and learning.

By following these steps, you can develop a growth mindset for lifelong learning. Remember that developing a growth mindset is a journey, not a destination. Continuously practice and cultivate your growth mindset to achieve your full potential.

Chapter 19: The Role of Spirituality in Mindset Development

In recent years, there has been growing interest in the role of spirituality in mindset development. Spirituality is often defined as the search for meaning and purpose in life beyond the material world, and can include beliefs in a higher power, religious practices, meditation, and mindfulness.

While spirituality is often associated with religion, it can also be a personal and individual journey. Developing a spiritual mindset can help individuals find inner peace, a sense of purpose, and a deeper connection to the world around them.

Here are some ways in which spirituality can play a role in mindset development:

1. Providing a sense of purpose and meaning: For many people, spirituality provides a sense of purpose and meaning in life. This can help individuals develop a more positive and growth-oriented mindset, as they are motivated by a larger sense of purpose.

2. Encouraging mindfulness and reflection: Many spiritual practices, such as meditation and prayer, encourage individuals to be mindful and reflective. This can help individuals develop a more present-focused mindset and become more aware of their thoughts and feelings.

3. Fostering compassion and empathy: Many spiritual practices

emphasize compassion and empathy for others. Developing a mindset that is focused on helping and serving others can help individuals develop stronger relationships and a sense of connection to the world around them.

4. Promoting gratitude and positivity: Many spiritual practices emphasize the importance of gratitude and positivity. Developing a mindset that is focused on gratitude and positivity can help individuals develop a more positive outlook on life and find greater happiness and fulfilment.

If you are interested in developing a more spiritual mindset, here are some steps you can take:

1. Explore different spiritual practices: There are many different spiritual practices, from meditation and mindfulness to prayer and yoga. Take the time to explore different practices and find what resonates with you.
2. Set aside time for reflection: Make time each day for reflection and introspection. This could be through journaling, meditation, or simply taking a few minutes to be still and quiet.
3. Practice gratitude: Make a habit of focusing on the positive things in your life and expressing gratitude for them. This can help shift your mindset towards positivity and abundance.
4. Seek out community: Finding a community of like-minded individuals can be a powerful way to support your spiritual journey. Consider joining a religious community, a meditation group, or a spiritual retreat.

By incorporating spirituality into your mindset development, you can cultivate a deeper sense of purpose, connection, and fulfilment in life.

Chapter 20: Mindset and Success: Achieving Your Goals with the Ideal Mindset- step-by-step course of action

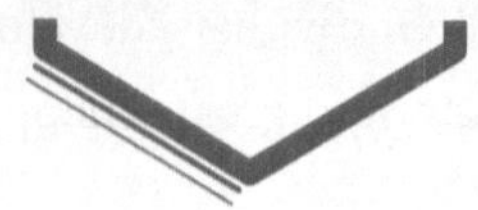

Developing the ideal mindset can significantly impact your success in achieving your goals. It is important to recognize that success is not just about accomplishing a task or reaching a destination, but it is also about the journey and the growth that comes with it. In this chapter, we will explore a step-by-step course of action for achieving your goals with the ideal mindset.

Step 1: Define Your Goals

The first step to achieving your goals with the ideal mindset is to define what you want to accomplish. This involves identifying specific, measurable, and achievable goals that align with your values and aspirations. Take the time to reflect on your personal and professional goals, and write them down in a journal or a goal planner.

Step 2: Adopt a Growth Mindset

Once you have defined your goals, it is important to adopt a growth mindset. This involves recognizing that failure is not a reflection of your worth or abilities, but rather an opportunity for growth and learning. Embrace challenges, view obstacles as opportunities, and persevere through setbacks with a positive attitude.

Step 3: Create an Action Plan

To achieve your goals, you need a plan of action. Break down your goals into smaller, manageable tasks and set deadlines for each one. This will help you stay focused and motivated, and track your progress along the way. Be flexible and willing to adjust your plan as needed, but stay committed to your ultimate goal.

Step 4: Cultivate Positive Habits

Developing positive habits can help you maintain the ideal mindset and support your efforts towards achieving your goals. Incorporate habits such as regular exercise, meditation, or journaling into your daily routine. Surround yourself with positive influences, and eliminate negative distractions that may hinder your progress.

Step 5: Stay Accountable and Seek Support

Staying accountable and seeking support can help you stay motivated and committed to your goals. Share your goals with a trusted friend, mentor, or accountability partner who can provide encouragement and hold you accountable. Celebrate your progress along the way and seek feedback to continually improve.

In conclusion, achieving your goals with the ideal mindset requires intentional effort and a commitment to personal growth. By defining your goals, adopting a growth mindset, creating an action plan, cultivating positive habits, and staying accountable, you can overcome obstacles and achieve success in all areas of your life. Remember to enjoy the journey, celebrate your successes, and continue to learn and grow along the way.

Chapter 21: Mindset for a Better World: Using the Ideal Mindset to Build a More Compassionate and Tolerant Society- a step-by-step plan of action

The world we live in today is facing numerous challenges, including poverty, inequality, environmental degradation, and social unrest. These challenges require a collective effort from individuals, organizations, and governments to address them. One way to approach these challenges is by developing an ideal mindset that promotes compassion, empathy, and tolerance. In this chapter, we will outline a step-by-step plan of action for using the ideal mindset to build a more compassionate and tolerant society.

Step 1: Cultivate Self-Awareness The first step in building a more compassionate and tolerant society is to develop self-awareness. Self-awareness allows us to understand our own biases, assumptions, and limitations, which are essential for developing empathy and compassion towards others. Self-awareness also helps us to identify the areas where we need to improve and develop new skills.

To cultivate self-awareness, it is essential to practice mindfulness, meditation, and self-reflection. These practices help us to become more present, observe our thoughts and emotions without judgment, and develop a deeper understanding of our inner selves.

Step 2: Foster Empathy and Compassion The second step in building a more compassionate and tolerant society is to foster empathy and compassion towards others. Empathy is the ability to understand and share the feelings of others, while compassion is the desire to alleviate their suffering.

To foster empathy and compassion, it is essential to practice active listening, seek to understand the perspectives of others, and engage in acts of kindness and generosity. These practices help us to develop a deeper connection with others, understand their needs and concerns, and develop a sense of empathy and compassion towards them.

Step 3: Develop Cultural Competence The third step in building a more compassionate and tolerant society is to develop cultural competence. Cultural competence refers to the ability to understand, appreciate, and respect the cultural differences of others.

To develop cultural competence, it is essential to engage with individuals from diverse backgrounds, seek to understand their cultural norms and values, and develop a curiosity for learning about different cultures. By developing cultural competence, we can build bridges across cultural divides and promote a more inclusive and tolerant society.

Step 4: Advocate for Social Justice The fourth step in building a more compassionate and tolerant society is to advocate for social justice. Social justice refers to the fair and equitable distribution of resources and opportunities within society.

To advocate for social justice, it is essential to become informed about social and political issues, engage in advocacy and activism, and support organizations and causes that promote social justice. By advocating for social justice, we can create a more equitable and just society that promotes the well-being of all individuals.

Step 5: Practice Mindful Communication The final step in building a more compassionate and tolerant society is to practice mindful communication. Mindful communication refers to the practice of communicating with intention, clarity, and compassion.

To practice mindful communication, it is essential to cultivate active listening skills, use non-violent communication techniques, and communicate with empathy and respect. By practicing mindful communication, we can reduce misunderstandings, conflicts, and promote a more harmonious and tolerant society.

In conclusion, building a more compassionate and tolerant society requires a collective effort from individuals, organizations, and governments. By following the step-by-step plan of action outlined in this chapter, we can cultivate the ideal mindset that promotes empathy, compassion, and tolerance. This, in turn, can lead to a more peaceful, just, and equitable society for all.

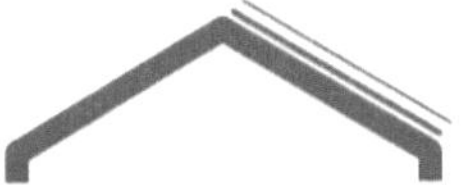

Chapter 22: Sacrificing Your Creative Humanity- At the Throne of Artificial Intelligence

Machines are not creative or imaginative, we humans have created machines with our creative intelligence. A machine can only do whatever it is programmed to do, it could do a mathematical equation, as swiftly as it can carry a tonne of materials from one part of the warehouse to another. The bottom line is that a machine can do much more than a human being could in one lifetime.

There are artificial intelligence open-source programs on the web that can generate an article, a poem, a short, story, a chapter of a novel, and perhaps even a full book, within a matter of minutes. There are A.I.-based art programs that can create fantastic art pieces with a few prompts, that can render these designs in a matter of seconds or minutes at the latest.

Everyone or almost everyone is dabbling with these new A.I. programs to see what they produce with the help of prompts, that tell the machine what they produce. We are sometimes amazed and sometimes embarrassed by the results. Depending on the instructions given to the program, the machine produces its materials, it could be a perfect poem or a perfect art piece. The rhyming is perfect in the poem, while the composition is almost perfect in the A.I.-generated image.

There are some writers who will produce artificially generated work, and publish it as their own work. There are a few artists who will also say that these A.I.-generated art pieces are their own creations.

Ultimately, we must realize that we are human creators. We can work with the assistance of A.I. programs, but we must not sacrifice our creative humanity, at the throne of artificial intelligence.

Chapter 23: Creating a Virtual Artificial Intelligence persona as a Writer

We are creating an artificial intelligence persona of ourselves, every time we write and publish online a literary piece of work, fiction or non-fiction. Our writings reflect our lives, our personalities, our thoughts, and our emotions. Therefore, logically, our writings embody who we are as humans.

We are creating a Virtual Artificial Intelligence representation of who we are as human beings, as we publish and share our literary works online- Is it scary or is that just the future of humanity and creativity?

There are AI writing programs, like "Emma Identity", which can evaluate a piece of writing and then compare it to the work of a real person, to know who wrote a piece of work. Perhaps, it would also be possible for such an A.I. writing program to create large bodies of literary works, based on a vast database of information and writings of any writer or published author in the future.

There may come a time when I can meet an A.I. version of myself, with the help of a quantum computer, who will think and write like me, based on my collected writings of over 2.5K stories written on Medium, in addition to my novels and other published writings. I am looking forward to the day when Warren meets A-I Warren, that would be the subject of another novel, LOL!!!

I am reminded of the movie, "Transcendence", with Johnny Depp, where he uploads his whole consciousness to an A.I. quantum computer system, that comes alive and embodies the mind of the man after he dies.

Perhaps there will come a time in the near future when the latest A-I generated literary works of Charles Dickens, Agatha Christie, Charlotte Brontë, Isaac Newton, Virginia Woolf, Jane Austen, Leonardo D Vinci, Sir Arthur Conan Doyle, and Mark Twain could be published, as their authentic works. Would you consider this invasion of the human mind, life, and creativity of a person unethical?

Chapter 24: The Symbiosis of AI- The Next Evolution

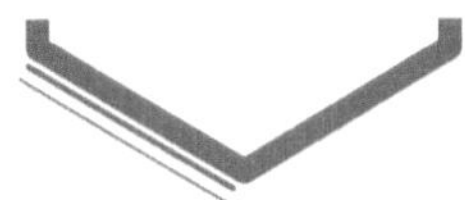

The future of marketing is one with artificial intelligence playing the field in a powerful and effective way. Customer behaviours, business models, sales processes, customer service options, marketing strategies will all be heavily influenced by artificial intelligence.

Driverless cars, technology to prevent the hacking of these driverless vehicles will increase. People will travel in these automatons without worrying too much, even when they have alcohol in their systems. The need for automobile insurance and breathalysers will disappear.

Efficiency and productivity will increase with the use of driverless vehicles. These new highly efficient automobiles will move faster and cover greater distances in a shorter time. Employees will increase their productivity, as they will move around for work much faster and get more done in a shorter time. A commuter could continue doing his or her work while traveling in an automated form of transport, knowing that he or she is safe in the vehicle.

Sales processes in the future will be enhanced and streamlined with the aid of artificially intelligent systems. Salespeople today pick up a phone to make a sales call or do a follow-up later. However, when artificial intelligence is present in the selling process, this will not be necessary. The A-I sales bot could analyse the tone of a customer and then provide feedback to the salesperson at the right moment to strike the deal. This would be just when the new customer sounds like or she is ready to sign the dotted line.

There is also the possibility that a sales bot could function as a human salesperson. However, if the customer detects that he or she is not being sold a product by a real person, they may stop interacting and the sale could be lost. This is a negative effect of having a sales bot taking full control of the selling of products until humans are comfortable being sold items by an automated sales force.

Online retailers ship products ordered by customers only after the order has been placed. Perhaps in the future, with the help of artificial intelligence products can be shipped directly to customers based on their shopping habits and preferences in the past. The products not needed by the customer will be returned back to the online retailer at no extra cost.

The greatest impact of AI on marketing will be in the industries of travel, banking, retail, and consumer packaged goods. A large amount of customer transaction data and customer attribute data are generated by these industries. This large quantity of usable data, with information from social media and data brokers, can be used by AI to create proper sales automated methods while taking into consideration privacy issues.

A framework needs to be developed based on AI processes, technologies, and features in order to evolve and revolutionize the role of AI working with human managers in the future.

Chapter 25: Artificial Intelligence merges with Publishing

Artificial Intelligence has been making great strides in several fields of human endeavour. The original fear that almost all people had, was that Artificial Intelligence would replace people is not true. In the real world, A.I. is doing the menial tasks, while humans do jobs that require human intelligence and emotion, which A.I. is not able to accomplish at present, to some degree.

In the future Artificial Intelligence will be present in all industries including the field of printing and publishing. There will come a time in the history of the world, when man and machine will work together in some form of cohesive harmony. The machines will not be taking over the world, yet.

In my novel, "Impostor Assassin", I have taken the reader into the world of futuristic publishing. I have envisioned a world where everyone needs to imagine, create and write their stories as a personal record and for the world of readers to enjoy.

In the world of the future, one conglomerate control the world through the media of writing and publishing. This colossus is opposed to the independent writer and publisher, seeking to destroy him and the auto-publishing programs he has created.

This publishing giant also starts to kill our Hero's family and so obliterate his self-publishing legacy he has given the world. Will independent writers and publishers of the future face a threat from established companies?

Chapter 26: An Enlightening Conversation- When A Writer meets Himself

There are two people sitting at a table. The first person is the teenage writer Bob Never-Writes, he is sipping a cup of coffee and doodling on a sheet of paper. Sitting across from him is an older man who resembles the teenage writer and he is Bob Always-Writes. The table at which the two writers, past and present versions of the same writer is in a parallel universe, where people can meet and greet, their past and future selves.

This parallel universe where it is possible to meet your younger or older selves is called "Paradise Space Café". Many writers visit this café, when they have questions for their future selves and when they want to enlighten their younger selves and request them to mend their ways.

Bob Always-Writes was a struggling writer and he was trying to tell his younger self to stop all his doodling as that led to him being a failure as a writer. He tried painting and drawing, but failed miserably. Bob Always-Writes was telling his younger self to keep a journal and write every day. He remembers that as a teenager he received so many fantastic ideas, but he did not write or publish them. All those stories that could have made him a bestseller today, were lost and adopted by other writers who gave concrete form to those illusive ideas.

Just as Bob Always-Writes was getting exasperated with the teenager Bob Never-Writes, the door of the Café opened and in stepped Bob-Barely-Writes. He was an elderly gentleman with white hair and he wore a designer suit. He was well dressed with his sparkling gold spectacles, and he exuded opulence and success.

The elderly Bob Barely-Writes went up to the table where the other two Bobs were sipping coffee and lemonade. He ordered champagne for the table. Bob Barely-Writes told the middle-aged Bob Always-Writes not to be so hard on the teenager Bob Never-Writes.

The middle-aged Bob Always-Writes was upset and he was eager to know the secret to the elderly Bob Barely-Writes success and good fortune. It is now that the most enlightening conversation takes place.

With a smile, as he sips his sweet champagne, the rich and famous Bob Barely-Writes says, "It is all about A.I. and meditation. I meditate every morning; I receive a bunch of fabulous stories from my A.I. mentor program that are soon converted into bestsellers. I make my billions and enjoy my success. The days of the struggling writer are a phenomenon best left in the past."

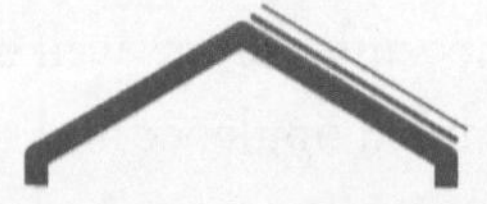

Chapter 27: AI Technology and Dementia

Researchers from the University of Exeter have studied data over a ten-year period on 15,300 patients who attended memory clinics in the US. The attendees were not facing any difficulties with their memory. Until two years later it was discovered that 1 in 10 attendees (1,568 attendees), during the period of 2005 to 2015, received a new diagnosis of dementia.

"The baby boomers are getting older and will stay older for longer. And they will run right into the dementia firing range. How will a society cope? Especially a society that can't so readily rely on those stable family relationships that traditionally provided the backbone of care?"

-Terry Pratchett

This 92 percent of accuracy in predicting who would develop dementia was possible with the assistance of machine-learning algorithms or artificial intelligence technological methods. According to Alzheimer's Disease International that was 55 million people worldwide living with dementia in 2020.

AI can not only accurately predict who will be diagnosed with Alzheimer's disease accurately, as well as increase the accuracy of the diagnosis. This will make quicker treatments possible. This is made possible when machine learning is used to study, research and analyse, patient information, lifestyle factors, cognitive tests, memory, and brain function.

"That's the thing with dementia. If you're with somebody who has a serious illness, you can usually talk to them, have a laugh every now and then — the person is still with you. With dementia, there's no conversation; there's no togetherness, no sharing."

-Judy Parfitt

Dementia is a syndrome, consisting of related symptoms that include memory loss, trouble speaking, understanding, judgment, movement, mood, mental sharpness, use of words, thinking speed, and difficulty doing daily activities.

Perhaps, with the use of AI technology, it will be possible to understand and control dementia in the future. Machine learning studies have hidden patterns in data and attempts to reveal who is most at risk of developing dementia.

"My husband is leaving me. No dramas, no slammed doors — well, OK, a few slammed doors — and no suitcase in the hall, but there is another woman involved. Her name is Dementia."

-Laurie Graham

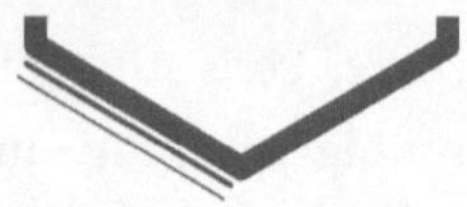

Chapter 28: The Miracle of Mind Cash

The day for making payments in notes and coins is gradually disappearing, they are now replaced with plastic card payments, which are now moving slowly, but surely to cryptocurrency. We are still not sure if digital currency will become the standard for trading in the decades and the years to come.

What if the day comes when it will be possible to pay for anything just by thinking about a product or a service that we wish to purchase? If this works, then we could just mentally have products and services available in our mental visual shop, where we could trade items.

Scientists have been working on the idea of linking our thoughts to machines. The linking of the human mind with the assistance of artificial intelligence has come a long way over the last few decades. A.I. has advanced in leaps and bounds.

The brain is a neurological network of nerve cells and tissues with electronic pulses being sent several billion times a second, which are similar to a computer managing data. According to scientists, there are approximately 100 billion neurons, with each firing 5 to 50 messages (action potentials) per second. The field of neuroscience has made a lot of astounding discoveries related to the immense power of the brain.

The day of Miracle Mind Cash is not too far away in my humble opinion. The day will come at some time in the future of human existence when it will be possible to earn, bank, and spend money using the power of our thoughts. Do you think that this could come about in the near or distant future and will it be advantageous or detrimental for the economies of the world?

Imagine the currency of the world, will be held in the minds of the population of the people of the world. Humanity will be in a powerful position for creating industries, generating wealth, and distributing wealth for the betterment of mankind. This will all be possible, with the power of thought, embedded in the brains of every living person, as a result of the collective electrochemical activities of all humanity.

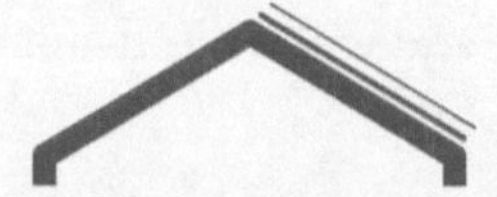

Chapter 29: Can a computer write Poetry?

I recently saw an interesting program on TED Talks it was a talk by Oscar Schwartz on computers writing poetry. The lecture was very illuminating. In it, Oscar tests the audience to see if they can tell the difference between a poem written by a human and one written by a computer program. It was easy for the audience to distinguish between the two samples at the beginning. However, it was difficult for the audience to know the difference at the end of the lecture when two poems were displayed.

The conclusion of Oscar's discussion was that the computer just reflects the work of the poet that is entered into its database for the algorithm to work on. If the works of William Blake are entered into a computer, it will produce poems based on the works of the poet. If the works of Emily Dickinson are entered into a computer, the work produced will only represent her type of writing and expressions. The computer is unable to produce anything different, from what is entered into its system.

A human on the other hand is capable of writing in different forms, with different expressions, and able to produce work that can resemble the work produced by a computer. The concept of "human", is one that is difficult to define, as some poets can write can humans do, while others can also write pieces of literature and poetry that resembles the work generated by computer systems and algorithms.

Chapter 30: The Last Writer- A Chronicler of Human History

Imagine that there are no people left in the world who want to write or enjoy the literary craft of writing, as it is now done by machines. If you want to read a novel, you can order one created by an artificial intelligence program. If you have the desire to hear a poem, you can order one to be tailor-made for you by an A.I. bot, that will write and recite it to you within five seconds.

What if you could have a novel written for you, with all the elements in the story that you want, it will be written for you within ten minutes, all you need to do is select the number of words. You could also tell the computer program to write a bestseller. In this futuristic world where no one has any need or desire to write, there is just one person who believes in the art of writing.

This last writer will have a large amount of work to do. He or she will need to record our human existence, for the future and for the benefit of mankind. Although there are millions of books written by A.I. programs, none of them will have the human factor and emotions locked into the words of every story, article, or poem.

The last human writer will need to be a chronicler of human history. He or she will write the history of mankind from the human perspective. There will come a time in the future, we writers can only hope, that mankind will abandon its dependence on artificial intelligence, especially in the creation of creative and artistic items, like paintings and literary pieces.

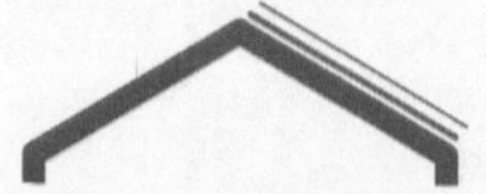

Chapter 31: Breaking Traditions in Literature and Art

When there is something that we do for a long period of time, it becomes a habit. A good habit is great, but a bad habit is hard to break. In society, there are customs and traditions that have been practiced for generations, so we just continue doing the same thing.

The case with traditions is that we do not question them, we just think to ourselves that it is the right thing to do. The times have changed and whether there are some ancient social traditions or ways of learning traditions or ways of working, we need to realize that things need to change.

A traditionalist is one who would not want things to change. I love traditions both old and new ones. Traditional writing and publishing are a few of the things that have undergone a transformation. The pandemic has changed the way that we work and live.

Traditional publishing has changed and so has art. With the creation of open-source writing, art, and publishing, so many things are changing in the world and it is sometimes hard to keep up. It is now possible to independently publish a book. It is now possible to automatically create an article, essay, or poem, with the help of artificial intelligence. It is also possible to create fantastic forms of digital art, with a few words and descriptions, whether you happen to be an artist or not.

Does the introduction of A-I-based writing and art depreciate the value of a writer's or an artist's work? Personally, I feel that real writers can express themselves from the heart like no artificially generated piece of work could. Somehow, an A.I.-generated piece of writing or art, looks perfect and it has a thousand little nuggets of information placed, that would not have been possible if composed by a human being. A machine can replicate the work of a human and make it appear as if composed by a human being.

I have always felt that an individual needs to make new paths in life. That is the best way for a person to get better at any skill or craft, including writing or art. A few well-placed descriptive words could generate an article, poem, story or novel, or an excellent piece of art, but that will in no way enhance the experience of the human creator.

As a writer and an artist, I believe that it is ultimately up to the writer or artist to choose the best form of creation, whether it is independent of artificial intelligence or completely created by A.I. and published as the writer's original work. Break traditions in life, but always do it with a conscience, as that is the best way to grow and develop as a human being in the 21st century.

Chapter 32: Techno Hub and the Meaning of Life

We are surrounded by technology of all types from iPhones, smartphones, to smart televisions and smart homes. Everything is available to us at the click of a button. We are now able to be in touch with the world and get any information we want in seconds.

Finding news and information which usually took an extraordinary time to locate ten years ago is now available at our fingertips. Project reports can now be drafted, discussed, and finalized online within a matter of days. Projects can be approved and started in a matter of weeks.

Technology helps us to save a surprising amount of time. That same time is utilized on gaining knowledge, expertise as systems is digitized, improved, and made more efficient. Artificial Intelligence is playing a vital part in the modernization of science and technology in all spheres of life.

With the advent of digital, cryptocurrency, the decentralized currency system is now coming into play, which are bank-free methods of transferring wealth or ownership of any commodity, without needing a third party.

There are so many innovative scientific projects being introduced in the world every day, that it is hard to keep up with the changes. The latest news about the Internet from Space is the Starlink project from

Space X. After four days of beta testing, the beta testers reported that the internet worked flawlessly.

In the field of sleep tracker technology, Google released its Sleep Sensing gadget that tracks a person's sleep patterns, by measuring motion and noise by their bedside. It keeps track of when a person goes to bed, how long it takes to sleep, the number of times sleep is interrupted during the night, and how fast the sleeper breathes at night. However, there are certainly privacy issues that need to be sorted, when a person sleeps with Google.

We can look forward to more innovative gadgets and technology being introduced to the world. This year, like last year, the conference will not be held in Silicon Valley but will be online. It is possible that new iPhones, Intel processors, chips for Mac computers, self-driving cars, and smart headsets will be introduced to the world.

Google Maps is to start showing more eco-friendly routes so as to highlight trips with lower emissions and will be based on factors such as traffic and slopes. Technology is helping us to keep ourselves and our families safe.

Techno Hub: We are all familiar with our techno-hub at home and at work. This is the area where we store all our technology. Every day we take care of our tech, by charging them up for the day. Without being charged none of these smart gadgets would work. At the end of the day, we return back to the temple of Technology and return our gadgets to rest for the night. This techno-hub is the favourite temple to technology which we now visit at the start, during, and at the end of the day.

Modelling our Techno Minds: Our minds are synced to technology and we are quick to find answers to any questions we have. The human mind has been remodelled by technology. In a flash of minutes and seconds, we can get any job done, no matter where in the world we may be at the time. Our minds are modelled to turn to and utilize the latest technological apps and gadgets to do whatever we need in life.

There is the popular saying, that "there is an app for everything." Whether we wish to accept it or not, we want to think more like machines. Artificial Intelligence is what we seek to assist us in our lives every day.

The Meaning of a Techno Life: Ultimately, our life is so dependent on technology, that we are all caught in its cold embrace. We cannot turn our backs on technology or we will be lost in the world without it. What would be the meaning of life in the technological age that we live in?

In my opinion, the meaning of life in such an advancing technological renaissance is for us to find a way to live comfortably with technology. We always need to remind ourselves that we are humans and still need to get in touch with our human emotions and life purpose.

We are not living in an artificially intelligence-generated matrix or in a computer-generated game. We are human beings and we need to inculcate within us and in future generations our human values.

Chapter 33: Robots and artificial-intelligent weaponry on the battlefield

There is a war raging in Ukraine even as this article is written. The country, the cities, and its people are facing the devastations of war and the destruction of their lives. It can be assumed that some forms of artificial intelligence in weapons and battle systems are being used during this war.

In fact, these are just a few of the artificial intelligent weapons that are being used in the frontlines of the present Russia and Ukraine war:

Lethal autonomous weapons systems- weapons with the ability to select targets and kill people, without human oversight.

- TB2 drones, that can take off, land and cruise autonomously.
- "Lantset"- These are "kamikaze" drones: a "loitering munition", designed to attack troops and tanks.
- "Deepfakes"- These are very realistic videos, which are faked for the purpose of disinformation campaigns.
- A.I. could be used to analyse open-source intelligence coming out of Ukraine.
- Machine learning could be used to detect misinformation in communications.
- The implications of A.I. in the protection and use of atomic weapons and facilities.

The time has not yet arrived for A.I. soldiers and killer droids on the battlefields as we have seen in movies like "Star Wars", but the time is not too far away when it could be a reality.

A.I. researchers are well aware of and worried about the dangers of artificial intelligence in wars. It is now time for them, along with world leaders, war strategists, and scientists, to put measures in place so that artificial intelligence is not used to destroy more lives, cities, and countries.

We all can hope and pray that this war ends soon so that the cities and the country can be re-built and peace can return once more. Artificial Intelligence is one of the greatest wonders and achievements of man and it should be utilized for the benefit of humanity.

"If it takes 200 years to achieve artificial intelligence, and then finally there is a textbook that explains how it's done, the hardest part of that textbook to write will be the part that explains why people didn't think of it 200 years ago..."

-John Mccarthy- Father of Artificial Intelligence

Chapter 34: Present Danger to Popular Famous Artists Revealed

Artificial Intelligence Image Generators are copying the works of famous artists and making thousands of new images. There is panic now among these popular artists as their works are being duplicated with A.I. technology and they have no way of stopping it from being done.

One such artist is Greg Rutkowski, a polish artist, whose work is now being reproduced by A.I. which copies his style and his techniques to create work that resembles his art. Greg creates fantasy images with Dragons and epic battles. Greg Rutkowski has now become a popular search in A.I. art, although he has never used it to generate art himself.

A.I. is now cloning the work of popular artists, by making multiple versions of their work. Will there be any form of legislation put in place so that this does not happen? Is A.I.-generated art as valuable as the original work of an artist? A.I. art in my opinion will also have value in the art market. One original image can be duplicated a hundred or more times, each with tiny differences, like in the case of NFT artworks.

What would we as writers do if such a thing occurs, with A.I. generators reproducing original literary works, that will have our voice, style and presentation? I doubt we will have control, although we have our intellectual rights as writers, as do other artists, to stop the production of such work. In the case of writers, it is a form of plagiarism. While in the case of artists, it would be art forgery.

How would you as a writer protect yourself from this type of plagiarism, where your stories, poems, and articles, are created by article and story generators in the future? In my case, I make certain to take my stories, articles, and poems, and compile them into books and e-books, as well as short courses. Defend your Intellectual rights as a creator and artist!!!

Chapter 35: Fiction: The Writer with Bionic Eyes

Her eyes were failing her and she could not see clearly anymore. This was affecting Trina's life as a writer and illustrator. Trina lived with her daughter and her family. Trina loved writing eight hours a day since she became a freelance writer and graphic artist. She was in her early fifties and her eyesight was quite poor.

It was the first of September, and Trina saw the advertisement that was to change her life. A leading A.I. company needed ten subjects to try their new bionic eyes technology for free. The volunteers would stay at the headquarters for six months, while they used the bionic eyes, which would be monitored by the eye specialists of the A.I. industry.

Trina signed up for the bionic eyes program. If the technology was suitable, the subject who was testing out the bionic eyes, would be allowed to keep the million dollar technologically advanced eyewear, which fitted comfortably over the patients' cornea after surgery was performed.

On the day of the surgery Trina was nervous. It was over before she knew it. The operation was fast and painless. A week later Trina started to use the new bionic eyes with all its features, which operated on simple mental and voice commands. Trina became unstoppable as a writer and graphic artist.

Whenever, the bionic eyed writer needed information on a topic, it would pop up on a 3-dimensional screen in front of her, which was a projection from her bionic eyes. Trina could now see all the information she wanted, while her vision was also enhanced.

Six months later after having successfully completed the medical trial project, she left the research facility with the bionic eye-pieces. There was an added benefit that Trina now enjoyed, which was her secret. She could "see" the past like it was happening in front of her eyes. The first time Trina visited Pompeii, she was amazed to see the people, the city, the social interactions, the culture, the religion and the city come alive, in visuals from the past.

Chapter 36: Does AI need to be destroyed? The AI Ethical Debate

The debating society of the University of Oxford, called the Oxford Union, recently held a debate where they challenged artificial intelligence to debate the ethics surrounding its own existence. The Megatron Transformer which is an AI supervised learning tool is based on the earlier work of Google and has been developed by an NVIDIA-based deep research team.

The Megatron possesses all of the knowledge of Wikipedia, it is trained on real-world data, with access to 63 million English news articles from 2016–2019, a large number of creative commons sources, and a connection to the 38 gigabytes of Reddit discussions. Megatron was definitely ready to meet the challenge.

This was a very interesting debate between humans and artificial intelligence. The topic of the debate was, "the house believes that AI will never be ethical." To which Megatron the artificial intelligence supervised learning tool responded, that AI can never be ethical as it is only a tool and can be used for good or for bad purposes. There is also no such concept of a good AI, but good and bad humans.

The final conclusion was that to avoid an AI arms race, there should be no AI presence in the world. This would be the ultimate defence against AI. The AI case was that artificial intelligence is not smart enough to be ethical. AI argued to remove itself from existence, as it is but a tool and can be used for good or bad reasons by humans.

The Megatron AI tool could not find a counter-argument to the motion, "data will become the most fought-over resource of the 21st century. AI was quick to inform us that they (artificial intelligence) would be able to see everything about a person, everywhere they go. It will all be stored and used in ways that no one can imagine at present.

Chapter 37: A.I. and Transhumanism

Transhumanism is a new way of thinking which theorizes that man can become more than just a human being with the help of technology. This use of technology goes to the extent where technology is integrated into the human body. Therefore, a man will become a combination of machines. This symbiotic union of man with technology will be the new evolved nature of man according to the philosophical movement called transhumanism.

The primary goal of Transhumanism is to move man from his position of being an ordinary human to an evolved and enhanced being. This can be achieved with the help of technology and artificial intelligence fused into the body of a man. Microchips, longevity, and the eradication of death are some of the objectives of the philosophy of Transhumanism.

With the help of human enhancement technologies, artificial intelligence, the new enhanced man will be a superhuman being capable of doing so much more in life. This will be possible when sophisticated technologies are widely available to modify and increase human intellect and physiology.

"Transhumanism is a class of philosophies of life that seek the continuation and acceleration of the evolution of intelligent life beyond its currently human form and human limitations by means of science and technology, guided by life-promoting principles and values." – Max More (1990)

The document referred to as the Transhumanist FAQ was developed in 1998 and finalized in 1999, by the work of leading members in the field of transhumanists.

What would our human future look like, when ordinary humans are surrounded by transhumanists, who are intellectually and physiologically superior? If these sophisticated technologies are available to all mankind it would help in the evolution of mankind with the use of artificial intelligence.

However, as we now look around at the world, I can see that we are living in a world of smart technology, where computers speak, phones with apps can do remarkable things for us. With the help of immersive technology, we are now able to re-create virtual environments for us to use for enjoyment, creative enterprises, learning, and gaming.

Has the Age of Transhumanism arrived, are we looking forward to an infinite future of an intellectually and physiologically superior human race?

Chapter 38: The largest Expo on Artificial Intelligence, 14–16 April 2022

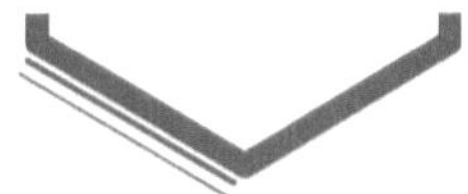

What if there was an event taking place somewhere in the world, where you could attend physically or remotely, which was only focussed on Artificial Intelligence? A place where the greatest minds in all fields of endeavour come together to ponder, discuss, display and provide information on A.I.

Welcome to the World Artificial Intelligence Cannes Festival. The purpose of the festival was to bring together individuals and businesses that were interested in and working with A.I. There is a virtual explosion of ideas on the innovative uses of artificial intelligence and the tremendous impact it plays in the world, societies, and cultures in the fields of science and technology. Industry leaders and decision-makers all come together to discuss advances and new ideas for the creative use of artificial intelligence in the world.

At this event, decision-makers and industry leaders came together to discuss the A.I. ecosystem, the emergence of responsible and ethical instruments, as well as the strong effects on economical, societal, and human needs.

It was possible to attend the three-day event physically and remotely. An individual could get a pass for the event and expect a wide array of events to take place. You could expect to find 10,000 practitioners, 150 exhibition companies, with 200 speakers on the subject of artificial intelligence. Your mind could have been enriched by all that you saw, heard, and experienced at the World A.I. Cannes Festival.

Chapter 39: AI will not replace Human Workforce

There is the myth that all human beings will be replaced by robots in the future. According to scientists, this is not true. Artificial intelligence will just be employed to do repetitive tasks which are usually done by humans. This in turn will free human workers to do more intellectual pieces of work in any organization.

Will there be an artificial intelligence workforce in the near future, possibly by 2030? If engineers, scientists, and merchants of industry are to be believed, such a thing will not occur in our future and we humans have no cause for concern. According to these experts in the fields of robotics, machine learning, and artificial intelligence, there will be a form of synthesis between AI and the human workforce, with new types of work being created in the future, for the benefit and advancement of human civilization.

As robots and other advanced forms of artificial intelligence are not and will not be as sophisticated as human beings, there is no threat of the human workforce being replaced by a robot army of workers. Machines only have the ability to perform the tasks that are programmed into their systems. They are unable to think, feel and act on the thoughts gained as a result of not possessing, human consciousness, thoughts, feelings, and wisdom, as a result of the human experience.

In fact, there will be a new evolution in the world of work, with new developments being made that will depend more on the human worker, aided by artificial intelligence. The best of both worlds, AI and humans will join to create a fusion of industrial and scientific fields, which will have a direct consequence on the nature of work, resulting in increased productivity and efficiency. AI will be used for the benefit of humanity, in the right hands of leaders and the masters of industry, or so we hope.

Chapter 40: Artificial Intelligence in Healthcare and possible advances envisioned

AI in Healthcare is a broad term used to describe machine-learning software and algorithms to mimic human cognition in the understanding, analysis, and presentation of complex medical data.

There are thousands of health and health care cases that can be resolved with the use of artificial intelligence medical systems. There are several new scientific initiatives encouraging entrepreneurs, companies, institutions, colleges, universities, and non-profits to create, develop and implement unique and innovative AI-assisted technology into the Health and AI Healthcare marketplace. These new AI medical companies are willing to partner with groups in creating, developing, and implementing new AI medical systems into the field of healthcare.

Natural Language Processing (NLP) systems in healthcare can analyse rough notes on patients, producing remarkable notes for the improvement of the condition of patients, by understanding quality and improving methods. The understanding of clinical documentation in the field of healthcare is one of the most common uses of NLP.

Could the next possible advance in AI technology in the healthcare industry save more lives and extend the human lifespan? It is possible that with the help of AI advances in the field of healthcare, an individual's body can be monitored constantly, while repairing systems, replacing and maintaining a well-balanced human operating system.

Microscopic medical tech, with the help of nanotechnology, can move through the human system. It will not be long before AI nano-tech creates an inner circuitry to improve the health of everyone on the planet. This may take a few decades or it could be sooner than we think.

Chapter 41: Will humanity lose its writers?

With the arrival of artificial intelligence, in all fields of human endeavour, including the literary field, there is tension and fear in the air. The common question on the minds and lips of people is if A.I. will replace human beings in the workplace and in all fields of human enterprise.

There are machines doing the work done by humans. Those repetitious tasks as well as mechanical jobs are now being done by machines. In the field of art, there are new A.I. programs that can create artistic masterpieces in a few seconds, based on ideas typed in by the user. Will A.I.-created art replace the need for art created by human beings? I do not think so, this will not happen in the future.

In the literary field, there are artificial intelligence programs that can write poems, essays, stories, and articles based on the information, like prompts, ideas, and creative suggestions that are fed into the machine. The work created by these programs is interesting to read and does resemble the work created by a human writer.

The important question is if humanity will lose its writers in the future. I do not think that writers will disappear. Writing like art is a basic creative talent that we humans possess. It is this form of expression, that helps us to understand and appreciate our human existence in the world. Even if there comes a time when artificial intelligence creates large bodies of literature, they will never compare to the literary work written by human writers, who live the pain, joys, defeats, and victories of this human existence.

Chapter 42: Turning my words into Art as a Storyteller

Recently I discovered a few A.I. Art generator websites like Midjourney, NightCafe and Leonardo.ai, which are websites that convert words or prompts as they are called into artwork. The artificially generated artwork on these websites is so amazing and I do not need to be a great artist or photographer or skilled with photoshop to create similar work.

I have over the last month been trying my hand at converting "prompts" into art. I have also looked at a number of videos on YouTube which have introduced me to the world of AI Art. I have started on this A.I. Art generation journey as a writer, an artist and as a Storyteller.

I realized when looking at the illustrations generated by these A.I. programs that they do tell a story. As a writer, I tend to "see" or visualize my stories and poems, as I write them. I can also add those same creative lines as prompts to these A.I. art programs to obtain truly amazing artworks.

I grew up reading Marvel, DC comics and graphic novels, thanks to my father who encouraged me with them. Naturally, I started to draw the illustrations I saw in the comic books, as a child at the age of six. I have been drawing all my life, but I am still learning the art.

As a storyteller I know the value of ideas and the opportunities to turn those visuals into great stories and poems, that people enjoy reading and which I love creating. I have generated so many A.I.

artworks over the past month and I do not intend to stop. Almost every picture I have created seems to tell me a story. As I look at the fantastic artworks on my screen, I can see ideas forming in my mind. The pictures seem to tell me a story or they seem to have the makings of some interesting stories.

I know that not many people like all these A.I. Art programs, that create art based on the works of real artists and that they can produce millions of such illustrations by users in seconds. My heart does go out to the artists, who are finding this a threat. I do hope that some form of compromise is reached between the creators.

these A.I. art generation programs and human artists, so that both can co-exist in peace. I have been converted to A.I. Art and I am a believer in the power of a picture to speak a hundred words.

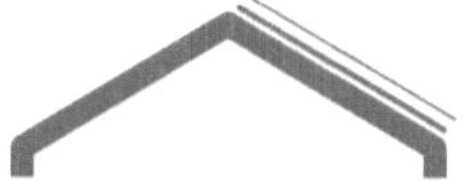

Chapter 43: Artificial Intelligence will not take over the World

Artificial Intelligence is going to take over the world and control mankind is just a myth, according to a few articles I have read by experts. Yet, we fear the machines and think that someday they will dictate our human existence and possibly destroy us. Perhaps, this is because of some of the ways in which artificial intelligence has been depicted in science fiction novels and in cinema, as destroyers of mankind. A good example of this is the "Terminator" movie and series.

Machines are just machines and only function with the help of the programs that are installed in their circuitry. Is A.I. friendly to humanity? Yes, you can get a friendly A.I. that is programmed with social interacting skills, like a robot designed to look like a human being in appearance and in mannerisms, that will smile at you as you approach and converse with you, just like a human being. The same human-looking robot will also watch your reactions and react to you accordingly.

Yet, there are machines designed to do work that could be viewed as harmful, when it crushes cars or machinery in a junkyard. Machines are programmed by human beings to do all types of work in the various fields of work that we have in industries.

Machines do not have conscious, subconscious minds, hearts, brains, and souls like we do and so are incapable of thinking or feeling like we humans do in life. Machines are not capable of destroying us consciously, as they do not have minds and souls. However, we can either prosper in life with the help of machines that increase productivity and efficiency or we can be sent to our extinction if the same machines are programmed to destroy life-sustaining systems. The common factor in both cases is that it is the human-designed program that will be responsible for the desired end result. In other words, do not get a mad genius or a dictator to program an army of machine systems to destroy the human race.

Artificial intelligence will not take over the world. However, man and machine can have a symbiotic relationship that will advance both mankind and machines for centuries to come, which will be beneficial for the human race. A.I. is not a threat, but a useful tool, for humanity's advancement and evolution.

Don't miss out!

Visit the website below and you can sign up to receive emails whenever Warren Brown publishes a new book. There's no charge and no obligation.

https://books2read.com/r/B-A-LFGF-JLHIC

BOOKS2READ

Connecting independent readers to independent writers.

Did you love *The Mindset for Living in a World with Artificial Intelligence*? Then you should read *Chasm of Creativity and Inspiration For Writers*[1] by Warren Brown!

[2]

The Chasm of creativity and inspiration is filled with stories and poems on a variety of issues, including essays on how you can become a better creative writer. The subjects covered in this collection will open your eyes, to your own imagination and creativity.

After reading just a few pages of this book, you will be inspired by the "idea keys" contained within its pages to write and keep writing. You will find that your Muse will be awakened and your mind will get new ideas. Every title of a literary piece in this book is a "key" for you to use and develop into your creative work.

---

1. https://books2read.com/u/mY8P9W

2. https://books2read.com/u/mY8P9W

Writing is a non-stop process and it takes time and effort. Great writers are not born, it is only with inspiration and dedication to the literary craft that they develop into notable writers. You may not win the Pulitzer Prize or the Nobel Prize for Literature, but you will write and gift your literary creations to the world.

Leap into the chasm of your own imagination and creativity, as you discover all the wonderful literary pieces you can create if you just believe in yourself as a writer. *Share your creative imagination with the world in the form of your literary artistic creations. There is no need to wait for the right time to start your journey on the "Writer's Way", start today and watch as your treasury of creations increase in volume, just by writing a minimum of three pieces a day, or even one poem a day, is a great place to start.*

Read more at https://warren4.wixsite.com/warren.

Also by Warren Brown

Prolific Writing for Everyone
On Writing Magic
The Writer's Creativity Cave
The Writer's Oasis
Castle of Ideas and Inspiration for Writers
Chasm of Creativity and Inspiration For Writers
Island of Creativity and Inspiration for Writers

Standalone
Supernova: A Collection of Science Fiction Short Stories
Instant Poetry App
The Power of the Storyteller- A Collection of Short Stories
Vintage Tales: Eurasian Short Stories
Impostor Assassin
Camelot Crypto 1- Crypto Genesis
Camelot Crypto 2- Crypto Odyssey
Camelot Crypto 3- Crypto Symbiosis
Camelot Crypto: Three Short Crypto-currency Stories
Three Christmas Coins: A Poem
The Christmas Dimension
Happy New Year
Festive Delights

Coulrophobia: Empire of the Clown King
Creative Vibes
Rewrite Your Story To Become The Hero
Pandemic Blasters
New Year Odyssey
Pandemic Blasters Omnibus
Travel Man
Monkey in Mind
Masquerade
The Marauders and Mavericks
Mystic Inspiration Prompts for Writers
Cafe of Creativity and Inspiration For Writers
Quick Guide to Increasing Sales for Your Magnetic E-Book
The Global Citizen: A Step-by-Step Guide to Living, Working, and
Thriving Anywhere in the World
The Mindset for Living in a World with Artificial Intelligence

Watch for more at https://warren4.wixsite.com/warren.

About the Author

Warren Brown is an Author who has written in several genres from fiction to non-fiction. Warren is a certified Life Coach and Hypnotherapist. Warren completed his Advertising and Copywriting training through American Writers and Artists Inc. (AWAI). I have been an Indie publisher for over eleven years now. I have been writing and publishing on the web since 1993. Website:

https://warren4.wixsite.com/warren

Medium:

https://warrenauthor.medium.com/

Substack:

https://warrenbrown.substack.com/

Read more at https://warren4.wixsite.com/warren.

9 798223 048046